TAO OF THOREAU

Mark Jefferson Bozeman

Copyright © 2022 Mark Jefferson Bozeman

All rights reserved

The characters and events portrayed in this book are fictitious. Any similarity to real persons, living or dead, is coincidental and not intended by the author.

No part of this book may be reproduced, or stored in a retrieval system, or transmitted in any form or by any means, electronic, mechanical, photocopying, recording, or otherwise, without express written permission of the publisher.

ISBN-13: 9798420843833
ISBN-10: 1477123456

Cover design by: Art Painter
Library of Congress Control Number: 2018675309
Printed in the United States of America

Introduction:

What is Tao of Thoreau?

The Tao: a mysterious force that powers the universe.

Henry David Thoreau: one of America's foremost philosophers, who found patterns in Nature that lead to growth, contentment and power.

By combining these two great spiritual paths, *Tao of Thoreau* creates an exhilarating examination of humanity and human potential. Matching Thoreau's ideas with Taoism leads the Seeker on the way of simplicity, harmony and positive action that develops mind, body and soul. Merging these philosophies makes *Tao of Thoreau* a map for the journey to enlightenment.

How can Tao of Thoreau help you?

In *Tao of Thoreau*, you will see one page labeled "Thoreau" and the next page labeled "Tao". The first is made of quotes from Thoreau's *Walden*. These are his own words, and by themselves offer wisdom to find a natural, spiritual and powerful way. The next page links Thoreau's words to Taoism, and offer a guide to using these ideas to grow happiness and power as you attune your spirit to Nature and Tao.

If you are reading this book, you are already a Seeker. It is my hope that it will help you become a Sage.

Thoreau

I went to the woods because I wished to live deliberately, to front only the essential facts of life, and see if I could not learn what it had to teach, and not, when I came to die, discover that I had not lived.

I wanted to live deep and suck all the marrow out of life, to live so sturdily as to put to rout all that was not life, to cut a broad swath and shave close, to drive life into a corner, and reduce it to its lowest terms, and, if it proved to be mean, why then to get the whole and genuine meanness of it. Or if it were sublime, to know it by experience, and be able to give a true account of it.

Tao

Thoreau begins his quest by radically simplifying his world. Moving to a cabin in the woods enables him to identify distractions and illusions. Being alone helps him strip his life down to find out what is important and true in the hopes of discovering a path that has meaning and value.

Realistically, most of us cannot separate from society. Still, Thoreau teaches the Seeker to identify parts of life that drain our energy, hold us back, and trip us up.

This is what he means by fronting "the essential facts of life." What is truly important? What desires are part of my path, and which pull me away from it? Thoreau and Taoism propose a radical freedom from distracting and destructive thinking, mindsets and actions.

Thoreau

Let us spend one day deliberately as Nature, and not be thrown off the track by every nutshell and mosquito's wing that falls on the rails.

Let us rise early and fast, gently and without perturbation; let company come and company go, let the bells ring and the children cry, determined to make a day of it.

Let us settle ourselves and work, and wedge our feet downward through the mud and slush of opinion, and prejudice, and tradition, and delusion and appearance, till we come to the hard bottom and rocks which we can call reality, and say: This is.

Tao

Thoreau sees that to become a Sage he must live each day without being sidetracked by trivial distractions. Trains wouldn't run if they were derailed by small things on the tracks. Similarly, Nature adapts to circumstances as they arise, unable to waste time in worrying. Paying the right amount of attention to things conserves energy and focus. This gives the Seeker a chance to act and react in proper proportion to the problem.

How to be part of life without being consumed by it? Try to be like the Tao Master, who:

Attends to the inner significance of things and does not concern himself with outward appearances. The Sage ignores matter and seeks the spirit.

Thoreau uses his "inner vision" to stop blindly accepting cultural and personal bias. Now he can open himself to how things really are, not how he or society wants them to be. "Question everything" is not the end of the thought. It is the pathway to distinguish the genuine from the fake.

Thoreau

Shams and delusions are esteemed for the soundest truths, while reality is fabulous. If men would steadily observe realities only, and not allow themselves to be deluded, life, to compare it with such things as we know, would be like a fairy tale.

When we are unhurried and wise, we perceive that only great and worthy things have a permanent and absolute existence, that petty fears and petty pleasures are but the shadow of the reality.

Tao

Temporary distractions and entertainments are just that. When we give them too much value, they are given more energy than they deserve. Taoism teaches that if you constantly meddle with affairs you cannot be free from trouble in your life.

Judgement is not the problem. Closing the mind after judging is. An open heart and mind always leave the chance for change and evolution.

Caught up in desire, we want to recapture a feeling over and over, wearing it thin and robbing it of its original joy and fascination. To paraphrase Lao-tzu, if you are controlled by your senses it is difficult to find peace.

Practice remaining centered in the true and lasting aspects of life, focused on the wonders of this world. Practice living in the lasting joy so many crave, which is around and within all of us.

.

Thoreau

I lived alone in the woods, a mile from any neighbor, in a house I built myself.

In most books, the I, or first person, is omitted. In this it will be retained. After all, it is the first person who is speaking. I should not talk so much about myself if there were anybody else I knew so well.

Tao

Thoreau did not pretend to be a hermit. A mile is not far. Yet it gave him enough space to eliminate social distractions in an attempt to find himself.

His point is that he's using "I" to not just talk of himself, but all people. Thoreau is able to expose an essential reality: great ideas, truth, and clear sight are a shared inheritance. Three thousand years before Thoreau, Lao Tzu "proved" Taoism by saying, "How do I know it is true? I look inside myself and see." These statements aren't arrogant because they are true for all of us.

This is shown in *Walden* when Thoreau says:

> *The oldest philosopher raised a corner of the veil from the statue of divinity; I gaze upon as fresh a glory as he did, since it was I in him that was then so bold, and it is he in me that now reviews the vision.*

Philosophers may put truth into words, but they do not own it: it is a gift to all. Encountering a truth in old, bold words refreshes and renews it, giving its power to a new generation of Seekers.

Thoreau

I do not wish to be any more busy with my hands than necessary. My head is hands and feet. I feel all my best faculties concentrated in it. The intellect is a cleaver; it discerns and rifts its way into the secret of things.

My instinct tells me that my head is an organ for burrowing, as some creatures use their snout and fore-paws, and with it I would mine and burrow my way through these hills.

I think the richest vein is somewhere here abouts; so by the divining rod and thin rising vapors I judge; and here I will begin to mine.

Tao

After leaving behind distractions, Thoreau begins his search for the hidden and mysterious force that the Chinese call the Tao. Though he did plenty of physical labor, his passion is clearly intellectual and spiritual. This is why he searches for this treasure with a "divining rod", because what he is looking for is divine, which is elusive. Lao-tzu told us:

We look at it, and we do not see it, we listen to it, and we do not hear it,
we try to grasp it, and do not get hold of it.

So how can we find the Tao? There is no book or class that can truly teach oneness and clarity, or how to find that flow we're supposed to go with. Yet thinkers like these have left behind trail markers for us to follow, though in the end the path is unique to each of us. Try thinking of the path as not something you can have, but something you can be.

Thoreau

If I wished a boy to know something I would not send him to some professor to survey the world through a telescope or a microscope, and never with his natural eye.

Which advanced the most by the end of a month, the boy who made his own jackknife from the ore which he had dug and smelted, or the boy who had attended the lectures on metallurgy at the Institute and had received a penknife from his father? Which would be most likely to cut his fingers?

I mean that they should not play life, or study it merely, but earnestly live it from beginning to end.

Tao

Thoreau understands that education, and the mind, are not as powerful without experience, and that learning alone does not lead to development. Like Lao Tzu said: "Continuing to grind an axe after it is sharp will soon wear it away." Though knowledge can lead to truth, action is living the truth. There is no better teacher than the real world. Being in moments, mindful of the present, leads to fuller development. This is when learning, practice and action all blend to make power.

Thoreau

What is a course of history, or philosophy, or poetry, or the most admirable routine of life, compared with the discipline of looking always at what is to be seen? No method or discipline can supersede the necessity of being forever alert. Will you be a reader, a student, or a seer?

To be a philosopher is not merely to have subtle thought, but so to love wisdom as to live according to its dictates, a life of simplicity, independence, magnanimity, and trust.

Tao

What does a seer see? Reality unchained by prejudice and bias. The Sage lives a simpler life by dealing with what is, and forgetting desires or what "should be."

Thoreau's definition of a philosopher is a near mirror to Lao Tzu's famous Three Treasures: simplicity, humility, and compassion. They both see that simplicity means understanding what life asks, and meeting those responsibilities without aggravation or complaint. Stay calm, focus on what is, meet challenges humbly and confidently, and be kind and generous. Be fully committed to life, staying in the moment because now is the only reality.

Thoreau

There were times when I could not afford to sacrifice the bloom of the present moment to any work, whether of the head or hands. I love a broad margin to my life.

Sometimes I sat in my sunny doorway from sunrise to noon, rapt in a reverie, in undisturbed solitude and stillness while the birds sang or flitted noiseless throughout the house, until by the sun falling in at my west window, or the noise of some wagon on the distant highway, I was reminded of the lapse of time.

I grew in those seasons like corn in the night, and they were far better than any work of the hands would have been. They were not time subtracted from my life, but so much more and above my usual allowance.

Tao

As it says in the *Tao Te Ching*, "a good traveler has no fixed plans and is not intent on arriving." Adaptability is key to remaining open to the moment. Perhaps Thoreau had goals for that day, but he is unafraid to put them aside and sit in his doorway, sinking into the blessings of the present. With no fixed plans it's easier to notice the opportunities that arise along the way. It is as if the traveler is not only traveling, but is also always arriving. If the goal of every journey is here and now, the traveler cannot get lost, nor can time be wasted on sidetracks.

Thoreau

    I did not read books the first summer; I hoed beans. The seed corn was given to me. This never costs anything unless you plant more than enough. I got twelve bushels of beans, and eighteen bushels of potatoes, besides some peas and sweet corn. The yellow corn and turnips were too late to come to anything.

    Making the earth say beans instead of grass, this my daily work.

Tao

Thoreau is learning about his new world in the woods and how to live by its rules. How much control does he need? How much food? What changes need to be made to live this life? These are the lessons of the Tao Master, who "is always skillful at saving things, and so does not cast away anything."

Humans change their environment. Thoreau strives to find just the right amount of change, and understands he is not prepared for everything because he is trying something new. Searching for balance, planning for simplicity, and knowing his responsibilities gives him a chance for success and contentment.

Thoreau

I learned from the experience of both years that if one would live simply and eat only the crop that was raised and raise no more than he ate and not exchange it for luxuries and expensive things he would not be tied to an ox, or horse, or cow, or pig.

I was more independent than any farmer, for I was not anchored to a house or farm but could follow the bent of my genius, which is a very crooked one, every moment.

Tao

The reward of minimizing work is gaining time. Thoreau is free to explore, wonder, or simply loaf around. Importantly, he learns to stop acquiring more and instead be content with less.

He also exposes one of life's subtle traps: things own us as much as we own things. To prevent this, minimize what needs care or attention, and so become free to roam the world and gain some of its wonderful, intangible benefits. Lao-Tzu says:

Be content with what you have; rejoice in the way things are. When you realize there is nothing lacking, the whole world belongs to you.

Thoreau

Men's capacities have never been measured; nor are we to judge what he can do by any precedents, so little has been tried. Whatever has been thy failure, "be not afflicted, my child, for who shall assign to thee what thou has left undone?"

We might try our lives by a thousand simple tests; for instance, that the same sun which ripens my beans illumines at once a system of earths like ours.

This was not the light in which I hoed them. If I had remembered this it would have prevented some mistakes.

Tao

Thoreau believes in us. Leaving behind our failings leaves nothing but potential. He stops plaguing himself with ambitions, realizing he cannot put achievement before action. Lao Tzu says that the Master "seems inactive" yet there is nothing left to be done. Ordinary people are always busy, yet there is always more to do.

The Taoist principal of non-action emphasizes being over doing. When the Sage is in the moment, living the action, then there is only being. The now is the place to get things done.

Remembering how small he is in the cosmos helps Thoreau keep things in context. As great a thinker as he is, as influential as he has become, he is just a tiny speck in the vastness. Any mistake he made is a pebble tossed into the Atlantic. The ripples are soon swallowed by the waves.

Thoreau

Men say to me, "I should think you would feel lonesome down there, and want to be nearer to folks." I am tempted to reply to such, this whole earth which we inhabit is but a point in space. How far apart dwell the two most distant inhabitants of yonder star? Why should I feel lonely? Is not our planet in the Milky Way?

This seems to me not to be the most important question. What sort of space is that which separates a man from his fellows and make him solitary? I have found that no exertion of the legs can bring two minds much nearer to one another.

What do we want most to dwell near to? Not to many men, the post-office, the barroom, the meeting house, but to the perennial source of our life, as the willow stands near the water and sends out its roots in that direction.

Tao

Trees grow where there is sustenance, sending roots to the water, branches leaning to the sun. Thoreau knows that people can choose actions that lead to decay and diminishment, or can be attracted to those who take rather than give. As much as others can add to life, they can also cause the kinds of distractions that endanger development. Lao Tzu had a way to guard against this:

> *Though surrounded with magnificent sights, the Sage lives in tranquility. Yet if he becomes restless, the Sage loses his root.*

True nourishment comes from aligning with the forces of Nature. The Seeker sees personal growth, realization of dreams, and attracting positive people as evidence that the roots are tapping into a pure source.

Thoreau

From exertion come wisdom and purity; from sloth ignorance and sensuality.

If you would avoid uncleanness, and all the sins, work earnestly, though it be at cleaning a stable.

Drive a nail home and clinch it so faithfully that you can wake up in the night and think of your work with satisfaction. Every nail driven should be as another rivet in the machine of the universe, you carrying on the work.

Tao

    Work done thoroughly and well can be reflected on with peace, because nothing is left undone. When labor is completed in such a manner, it follows Lao-Tzu's advice: "Do your work, then step back. The only path to serenity." When work is actually finished, then the Seeker can focus on the next job. The Seeker understands what the *Tao Te Ching* says of the Master, "When her work is done, she forgets it. That is why it lasts forever." A Sage's work sinks seamlessly into the universe.

Thoreau

When it stormed before my bread was baked, I fixed a few boards over the fires, and sat under them to watch my loaf, and passed some pleasant hours in that way.

I made no haste in my work, but rather made the most of it. I am convinced, both by faith and experience, that to maintain oneself on this earth is not a hardship but a pastime, if we will live simply and wisely.

Tao

The *Tao Te Ching* says it this way:

The Master does his job and then stops. He understands that the universe is forever out of control, And that trying to dominate events goes against the current of the Tao.

Thoreau allows the rain to frame his day. Instead of getting annoyed, he adapts. Adaptation conserves energy; anger and frustration waste it. Going with the flow of events keeps the Sage rooted in the power of the moment, even if all that is required is a little patience.

Thoreau

My dwelling was small, and I could hardly entertain an echo in it; but it seemed larger for being a single apartment and remote from neighbors.

I would observe, by the way, that it costs me nothing for curtains, for I have no gazers to shut out but the sun and moon, and I am willing that they should look in.

I had three pieces of limestone on my desk, but I was terrified to find that they required to be dusted daily, when the furniture of my mind was undusted still, and I threw them out the window in disgust.

A lady once offered me a mat, but as I had no room to spare within the house, nor time to spare within or without to shake it, I declined, preferring to wipe my feet on the sod before my door.

It is best to avoid the beginning of evil.

Tao

Just as large things such as houses require effort and attention, so do the small things. For Thoreau, the prospect of dusting paperweights weighs him down. Avoid "the beginning of evil" by taking time and wisely selecting what requires attention. Thus, when the Seeker takes on something new, he or she is ready to bring the energy and focus required, and avoids the weight of an unexpected burden.

Thoreau

Every morning is a cheerful invitation to make my life of equal simplicity, and innocence, with Nature herself. While I enjoy the friendship of the seasons nothing can make life a burden to me. The gentle rain which waters my beans and keeps me in the house today is not drear and melancholy, but good for me too.

Nothing can compel a simple and brave man to a vulgar sadness. If all were to live as simply as then I did, thieving and robbery would be unknown. These take place in communities where some have got more than is sufficient while others have not enough.

I will not plant beans and corn with so much industry another summer, but such seeds as sincerity, truth, simplicity, faith, innocence.

Tao

One of the closest parallels between the *Tao Te Ching* and Thoreau is in this passage. Although there are various translations of the Three Treasures, the three most common are simplicity, humility and compassion.

A simple, calm and open existence can bring personal peace, and influence others to find peace for themselves. The closer Thoreau comes to the simplicity of Nature, the more he takes possession of the truly free gifts of this world.

Others are attracted to this, though they may not even know it; they align themselves to this energy unconsciously, as leaves turn to the sun.

Thoreau

Men say, "With kindness aforethought go about doing good."

If I knew for a certainty that a man was coming to my house with the conscious design of doing me good, I should run for my life.

If I were to preach at all in this strain, I should say, rather, set about being good.

Tao

Thoreau and the Taoists realize the difference between being good and doing what you believe is good for others. Doing good is often based on a set of fixed ideals or morals, which can prevent seeing what is really needed because the results have to conform to a certain world view. Chaung-tzu warns us: "You delight in doing good, and your natural kindness is blown out of shape. You delight in righteousness, and you become righteous beyond all reason."

Sincere goodness works for neither reward nor a particular outcome. A truly good person is an example for others to emulate. As Lao-tzu put it: "A good man is a bad man's instructor." Be attuned to the needs of others, willing to do for others as you would do for yourself.

Thoreau

 There are thousands hacking at the branches of evil to one who is striking at the root, and it may be that he who bestows the largest amount of time and money on the needy is doing the most by his mode of life to produce that misery which he strives in vain to relieve.

 Be sure that you give the poor the aid they most need, though it be your example which leaves them far behind. If you give money, spend yourself with it, and do not merely abandon it to them.

Tao

To truly defeat evil and promote good, society must delve to the source of the problem and solve it there. The same is true for the Seeker, who must be brutally honest about the evil inside to fix it. Again, it is best to see the problem for what it is, and not judge it based on preconceived ideas or codes. In the words of the *Tao Te Ching:*

> *The Sage focuses on reality and not shadow, and dwells with the fruit and not with the flower. Walking the path of the Sage means seeing to the depth of things, good or bad.*

Seeing the root of goodness helps us understand how to be truly good; finding the source of evil means we can uproot it, so it struggles to grow again.

Thoreau

I should not subtract anything from the praise that is due to philanthropy, but merely demand justice for all who by their lives and works are blessing on all mankind.

I do not value chiefly a man's uprightness and benevolence, which are his stem and leaves. I want the flower and fruit of a man; that some fragrance be wafted over from him to me, and some ripeness flavor our intercourse.

His goodness must not be a partial and transitory act, but a constant superfluity, which costs him nothing and of which he is unconscious.

Tao

What works for society works for the individual. Goodness like this is the same as embodying the Tao, which "since it is merged with all things and hidden in their hearts, it can be called humble. It isn't aware of its greatness; thus it is truly great." Merging into the flow of the Tao helps the Seeker to feel the right action in work, in play, and with people. As Chaung-tzu says, such a person "in whom Tao acts without impediment harms no other being by his actions yet he does not know himself to be 'kind', to be 'gentle'..." In this way goodness and simplicity merge into being, and action becomes effortlessly positive, naturally helpful, and genuinely modest.

Thoreau

Who knows what sort of life would result if we had attained to purity? If I knew so wise a man as could teach me purity I would go to seek him forthwith.

He is blessed who is assured that the animal is dying out in him, day by day, and the divine being established. Man flows at once to God when the channel of purity is open.

Our whole life is startlingly moral. There is never an instant's truce between virtue and vice. Goodness is the only investment which never fails.

Tao

The reason goodness cannot fail as an investment is because it is its own reward. The results of goodness are so obvious and so pure that it is hard to mistake them for anything else. Another signal of being on the right path is that good acts tend to recharge us rather than tire us out. Thus, it is said that the "Master can keep giving because there is no end to her wealth." The Sage's wealth is the Tao, the energy in all things; it is a well that does not run dry.

Thoreau

It is an interesting question how far men would retain their relative rank if they were divested of their clothes. Could you tell surely of any company of civilized men which belongs to the most respected class?

Beware of all enterprises that require new clothes, and not rather a new wearer of clothes. If there is not a new man, how can the new clothes be made to fit?

Tao

This new person might wonder, "Life or wealth, which do you hold more dear?"

The well-dressed person may be the worst person, while the humbly clothed is closer to answers so many seek. Being fulfilled, not worrying too much, rejoicing in the world as it is: these are some of the ways to be a "new man." Embodying these ideas leads to the conclusions of Chuang-tzu, who saw that "rank and reward have no appeal" and "disgrace and shame" hold no fear because hard work, integrity and goodness will eventually overcome the pain that comes with mistakes.

Thoreau

A man is rich in proportion to the number of things which he can afford to let alone. Superfluous wealth can buy superfluities only. Money is not required to buy one necessary of the soul. It is life near the bone where it is sweetest.

Tao

Life near the bone is a wonderful starting point for the Seeker. Focus on what is important: it exposes the trivial for what it is, laying bare what is most meaningful and deserves attention and energy.

Thoreau

The luxury of one class is counterbalanced by the indigence of another. The mason who finishes the cornice of a palace returns at night to a hut.

The setting sun is reflected from the windows of the almshouse as brightly as from the rich man's abode. You may perhaps have some pleasant, thrilling, glorious hours, even in a poorhouse. I do not see but a quiet mind may live as contentedly there as in a palace.

However mean your life is, meet it and live it; it is not so bad as you are.

Tao

Though the disparities between classes are real, a person who has the necessities of food, shelter and clothing still has an opportunity to be happy. True wealth is made up of much more than money and objects.

This passage reflects the Taoist idea: "He does not struggle to make money and does not make a virtue of poverty." Thoreau believes that poor people can enjoy many of life's fruits. The point being that once money is removed as the main component of happiness, other possibilities emerge as the source of riches.

Thoreau

    Of a life of luxury the fruit is luxury. Shall we always study to obtain more of these things, and not sometimes to be content with less? Most luxuries are not only indispensable, but positive hindrances to the elevation of mankind.

    When he has obtained those things which are necessary to life, there is another alternative than to obtain the superfluities; and that is, to adventure on life now, his vacation from humbler toil having commenced.

Tao

Lao-tzu asks us:

Fame or integrity: which is more important?
Money or happiness: which is more valuable?

While the questions seem obvious, the answers are not. This is not an "either/or" choice, but an understanding of the important distinction between the two. Integrity and happiness are more important and valuable than money and fame. These philosophers caution that money and fame only provide money and fame, while happiness and integrity are valuable beyond measure.

Luxuries bring problems with their benefits. There are worries that things might be ruined, stolen or lost. People may become jealous of what they don't have, or the owners suspect them of jealousy, making thoughts twist. With less focus on wealth or social standing comes less worry, and more opportunity to invest in what brings true happiness: goodness, freedom and love.

Thoreau

I do not mean to prescribe rules to strong and valiant natures, who will mind their own affairs whether in heaven or hell, and perchance build more magnificently and spend more lavishly than the richest, without ever impoverishing themselves; nor to those who find their encouragement and inspiration in precisely the present condition of things, and cherish it with the fondness and enthusiasm of lovers.

I have in my mind that seemingly wealthy, but most terribly impoverished class, who have accumulated dross, and have forged their own golden or silver fetters. But mainly to the mass of men who are discontented, and are idly complaining of the hardness of their lot, or of the times, when they might improve them.

Tao

To Thoreau, this feeling of discontent doesn't come from the difficulty of someone's life, but the perception of how his or her life should be different and better. Constantly feeling that life must be improved, refined, revised, and reformed, means never being able stop and enjoy our achievements.

These philosophies teach the Seeker to let go of the feeling that there always must be more and gain the power to really change things. Chuang-tzu knew this power:

When he is beyond form and semblance, beyond "this" and "that," where is the comparison with another object? Where is the conflict? What can stand in his way?

Thoreau

Men labor under a mistake. They are employed, laying up treasures which moth and rust will corrupt and thieves break through and steal. Life's finer fruits cannot be plucked by them. Their fingers, from excessive toil, are too clumsy and tremble too much for that.

He has no time to be anything but a machine. How can he remember well his ignorance, which his growth requires, who has so often to use his knowledge?

The finest qualities of our nature, like the bloom on fruits, can be preserved only by the most delicate handling.

Tao

Lao Tzu knew "if you overvalue possessions, people begin to steal." Neither the Taoists nor Thoreau would say that it's wrong to have and enjoy things, but when it is forgotten they are things, merely, and that they should not be given more esteem than they deserve, then the Seeker has stepped off the path of wisdom.

Chuang-tzu warns:

Those that think that wealth is the proper thing for them cannot give up their revenues; those that seek distinction cannot give up the thought of fame; those that cleave to power cannot give the handle of it to others. While they hold their grasp of those things, they are afraid of losing them. When they let them go, they are grieved and they will not look at a single example from which they might perceive the folly of their restless pursuits.

The other option is to work a little less, and spend more time pursuing life's free treasures like thinking, Nature, love, rest, and freedom. These treasures cannot be stolen but can be shared.

Thoreau

If you are a seer, whenever you meet a man you will see all that he owns and much that he pretends to disown, even to his kitchen furniture and all the trumpery which he saves and will not burn, and he will appear to be harnessed to it and making what headway he can.

The incessant anxiety and strain of some is a well-nigh incurable form of disease. We are made to exaggerate the importance of what work we do, and yet how much is not done by us!

Why should we live with such hurry and waste of life? We are determined to be starved before we are hungry.

Tao

Thoreau's understanding of property is reflected and expanded in the words of Tao master Chaung-tzu:

When he tries to extend his power over objects, those objects gain control of him. He who is controlled by objects loses possession of his inner self... Prisoners in the world of objects, they have no choice but to submit to the demands of matter! They are pressed down and crushed by external forces: fashion, the market, events, public opinion. Never in a whole lifetime do they recover their right mind! What a pity!

There is nothing wrong with work. Possessing things is not evil. The point is to balance them with what makes life full. What many see as having less the Seeker and the Sage see as being open to so much more.

Thoreau

We are in great haste to construct a magnetic telegraph from Maine to Texas; but Maine and Texas, it may be, have nothing important to communicate. As if the main object were to talk fast and not talk sensibly.

We are eager to tunnel under the Atlantic and bring the old world some weeks nearer to the new; but perchance the first news that will leak through into the broad, flapping American ear will be that the Princess Adelaide has the whooping cough.

Our inventions are wont to be pretty toys, which distract our attention from serious things. They are an improved means to an unimproved end.

Tao

The *Tao Te Ching* offers another choice:

> *They will be satisfied with their food.*
> *Delighted in their dress;*
> *Comfortable in their dwellings;*
> *Happy with their customs.*
> *Though the neighboring states are within sight*
> *And their roosters crowing and dogs barking;*
> *The people will not go there their whole lives.*

These aren't really admonitions against travel, or warning about the dangers of communication across great distance. It is a reminder that the problems and triumphs of our neighbors are the same as the weddings or tragedies of Lords and Ladies from far off lands, or actors and other performers. By focusing on genuine interaction and communication, on being truly present in the life of our home, the trials and tribulations of those far away may become trivial in comparison to those who are so close, whose lives impact ours and have more meaning to us.

Thoreau

 Hardly a man but when he wakes holds up his head and asks, "What's the news? Tell me anything new that has happened anywhere on this globe," and he reads over his coffee that a man has had his eyes gouged out this morning.

 Never dreaming the while that he lives in the dark unfathomed mammoth cave of this world, and has but the rudiment of an eye himself.

Tao

Thoreau was probably thinking of Plato's famous "Allegory of the Cave," which is partly about eliminating illusions to discover the higher, spiritual aspects of life. Being enthralled by news of the shallow makes it difficult to reach great depth. In Plato's allegory, each time a man evolves he emerges blinking into the light; his eyes needing time to adjust to the greater reality he has entered.

Chuang-tzu said, "Men honor what lies within the sphere of their knowledge, but do not realize how dependent they are on what lies beyond it." These thinkers saw that awareness of greater realities is a revolution in consciousness. This revolution can happen repeatedly, enlightening and deepening the Seeker.

Thoreau

I am sure I never read any memorable news in a newspaper. If we read of one man robbed, or murdered, or killed by accident, or one house burned, or one vessel wrecked, or one cow run over on the Western Railroad, or one mad dog killed, we never need to read another. One is enough.

If you are acquainted with the principle, what do you care for a myriad instances and applications? To a philosopher, all news, as it is called, is gossip.

I delight to come to my bearings, not walk in procession with pomp and parade but to walk even with the Builder of the universe. Not to live in the restless, nervous, bustling, trivial Nineteenth Century, but stand or sit thoughtfully while it goes by.

Tao

This is similar to the *Tao Te Ching,* which says:

The Master sees things as they are, without trying to control them. She lets them go their own way and resides at the center of the circle.

The sage can rest by understanding what is truly important. Clear vision reduces the influence of transient events. The settled mind "perceives the universal harmony, even amid great pain," because "peace in the heart" has been achieved. Reflecting the perfection of the Tao, the Sage becomes a mirror for the "bustling, trivial" world to see itself and, perhaps, slow down and evolve.

Thoreau

In accumulating property for ourselves or our posterity, in founding a family or state, or acquiring fame even, we are mortal; but in dealing with truth we are immortal, and need fear no change or accident.

The oldest philosopher raised a corner of the veil from the statue of divinity; and still the trembling robe remains raised, and I gaze upon as fresh a glory as he did, since it was I in him that was then so bold, and it is he in me that now reviews the vision.

Tao

We all have the ability to be a Sage, to raise the same veil that Thoreau raised. Truth and the Tao last forever. Each time a person discovers the truth and finds the path of the Tao, he or she becomes one with that immortality. Thoreau, Chuang-tzu and Lao Tzu are no better than you and I; they found a way that worked for them, and showed it to us. If we see answers to our questions in their words, then we become like them, joining them in the timelessness of truth.

The enlightenment so many seek outside themselves is already within them.

Thoreau

It is true, I might have resisted forcibly with more or less effect, might have run "amok" against society, but I preferred that society should run "amok" against me, it being the desperate party.

It is for a man to maintain himself through obedience to the laws of his being, which will never be one of opposition to a just government, if he should chance to meet with one.

Tao

In "Civil Disobedience", Thoreau wrote, "That government is best which governs least." Self-government is best because it becomes unnecessary for there to be so much interference from political power.

Lao Tzu put it this way:

> *The people are hungry because taxes are too high. Because their officials meddle with affairs, the people are hard to rule.*

Being trusted, perhaps more would want to maintain that trust. The ability to criticize our own nature and correct our own flaws is the best governance there is.

Thoreau

While civilization has been improving our houses, it has not equally improved the men who are to inhabit them. It has created palaces, but it was not so easy to create noblemen and kings.

Before we can adorn our houses with beautiful objects, the walls must be stripped, and our lives must be stripped, and beautiful housekeeping and beautiful living be laid for foundation: now a taste for the beautiful is most cultivated out of doors, where there is no house and no housekeeper.

I would rather sit in the open air, for no dust gathers on the grass, unless where man has broken ground.

Tao

This "beautiful housekeeping and beautiful living" would look like this:

The Tao does nothing, so there is nothing it does not do. If powerful people were able to maintain it, all things would become developed. This simplicity will end desire, and if desire is absent there is quietness. All people will be satisfied.

Thoreau

Nations are possessed with an insane ambition to perpetuate the memory of themselves by the amount of hammered stone they leave. What if equal pains were taken to smooth and polish their manners? One piece of good sense would be more memorable than a monument as tall as the moon.

It should not be by their architecture, but why not even by their power of abstract thought, that nations seek to commemorate themselves? How much more admirable the Bhagavad-Gita than all the ruins of the East? Towers and temples are the luxuries of princes. A simple and independent mind does not toil at the bidding of any prince. Genius is not a retainer to any emperor, nor is its material silver, gold, or marble.

With a little more wit we might use these materials so as to become richer than the richest now are, and make our civilization a blessing.

Tao

Indeed, Thoreau learned from the Bhagavad-Gita that, "To the illumined man or woman, a clod of dirt, a stone, and gold are the same." The material they are made of is the Tao.

All of this advice works equally well for people and for societies. The two have similar problems: the tendency to be obsessed with the superficial and the showy, and a difficulty in seeing their own flaws. Thoreau would prefer nations and people like this:

A great nation is like a great man: when he makes a mistake, he realizes it. Having realized it, he admits it. Having admitted it, he corrects it. He considers those who point out his faults as his most benevolent teachers.

Thoreau

I desire that there may be as many different persons in the world as possible; but I would have each one be very careful to find out and pursue *his own* way, and not his father's or his mother's or his neighbor's instead.

There is not one of my readers who has yet lived a whole human life. The life in us is like the water in a river. It may rise this year higher than man has ever known it, and flood the parched uplands.

Tao

Just as a desert blooms after a rainfall, Thoreau talks of people having the ability to renew, grow deeper roots and branch out higher. Acting as the Tao, we imitate water. "The highest goodness is like water. Water is good to all things. It stays in places which others despise." Growth is strongest and steadiest when it follows the right path. Allowing people to develop in their own way makes a society that is constantly refreshing itself and that is united by the strength and goodness of each individual.

Thoreau

What little true cooperation there is, is as if it were not; being a harmony inaudible to men. If a man has faith he will cooperate with equal faith everywhere; if he has not faith, he will continue to live like the rest of the world, whatever company he is joined to.

I think that we may safely trust a good deal more than we do. Could a greater miracle take place than for us to look through each other's eyes for an instant?

Tao

Thoreau sees this cooperation and trust in Nature. Everything is connected; each part dependent on the rest. Humans are like this, but many are unaware of it. Trust would come by looking through each other's eyes because we would see that we share the same needs, desires and wishes.

The Sage understands this level of trust, even though many would consider it dangerous, even insane. But the Sage is not like everyone else:

To those who are good, I am good; and to those who are not good, I am also good, and thus all get to be good.

Thoreau

I sat at a table where rich food and wine were in abundance, but sincerity and truth were not; and I went away hungry. They talked to me of the age of the wine and the fame of the vintage; but I thought of an older, a newer, and a purer wine, of a more glorious vintage, which they had not got, and could not buy.

Rather than money, than love, than fame, give me truth.

Tao

In the words of Chuang Tzu:

Love of colors bewilders the eyes, and it fails to see right. Love of harmonies bewitches the ear, and it loses its true hearing. Love of perfumes fills the head with dizziness. Love of flavors ruins the taste. Desires unsettle the heart until the original nature runs amok.

It is in "the original nature" that Thoreau seeks truth. Riches and good wine are wonderful until they become traps. Is the vintage of the wine a definition of refined taste or a desire for status? Is wealth an indication of hard work or of needs that cannot be fulfilled? Because truth and the Tao do not change even as wine sours and food goes bad, it is best to enjoy the things that are temporary while staying centered in what lasts.

Thoreau

Why should we be in such desperate haste to succeed, and in such desperate enterprises? If a man does not keep pace with his companions, perhaps it is because he hears a different drummer. Let him step to the music that he hears, however measured or far away.

It is not important that he should mature as soon as an apple-tree or an oak. Shall he turn his spring into summer? Do not seek so anxiously to be developed, to subject yourself to many influences, to be played on; it is all dissipation.

Humility, like darkness, reveals the heavenly lights.

Tao

The drumbeat is not only the "far away" of unique behavior, but also the "measured" beat of those who like to follow the rules, and the rhythm of everything in between. Thoreau wants everyone listening to their own music, and not to feel coerced to follow another's. Chuang-tzu said it like this:

He goes his way without relying on others and does not pride himself on walking alone. While he does not follow the crowd, he won't complain of those who do.

Nature develops at the pace appropriate for it; seasons follow seasons as they should. A settled person, within a settled society, grows at the speed most fitting for his or her nature. It is wrong to want spring to be summer because "rushing into action, you fail. Forcing a project to completion, you ruin what was almost ripe." Listen to the beat, be humble in following it, and gain a chance to walk with the divine.

Thoreau

In a pleasant spring morning all men's sins are forgiven. Such a day is a truce to vice. While such a sun holds out to burn, the vilest sinner may return. Through our own recovered innocence we discover the innocence of our neighbors.

Alert and healthy natures remember the sun rose clear. It is never too late to give up our prejudices.

Tao

Lao Tzu saw renewal as "return." Here is what he said:

When things have displayed their luxuriant growth, we see each of them return to its root. This returning to their root is what we call the state of stillness. Going back to the origin is called peace; it means reversion to destiny. Reversion to destiny is called eternity. He who knows eternity is called enlightened.

Renewal is a great force of Nature. It teaches that each moment provides a chance to change, reform and grow. Each return refreshes us, and extends our journey within enlightenment.

I say "within" above because the more I study these ideas, the more sure I become that enlightenment is not an end. Those on the enlightenment path are already experiencing its profound insights and power. Enlightenment has levels, and each one reached opens the vista for the next.

Thoreau

We should be blessed if we lived in the present always, and took advantage of every accident that befell us, like the grass which confesses the influence of the slightest dew that falls on it; and did not spend our time in atoning for the neglect of past opportunities.

We loiter in winter while it is already spring.

Tao

Earlier, Thoreau warned us not to try to turn spring into summer; here he warns us not to obsess on the past. Lao Tzu said:

> *Why was it that the ancients prized this Tao so much? Because it could be got by seeking for it, and the guilty could use it to escape the stain of guilt. This is the reason why all under heaven consider it the most valuable thing.*

Learn from mistakes and missed opportunities and apply this learning going forward. Practice forgiving yourself, especially if you have accepted the lessons from your mistakes. Forge forward with this learning, determined to make a new day and a new you.

Thoreau

The true harvest of my daily life is somewhat as intangible and indescribable as the tints of morning or evening. It is a little stardust caught, a segment of the rainbow which I have clutched.

If the day and the night are such that you greet them with joy, and life emits a fragrance more like flowers and sweet-scented herbs, is more elastic, more starry, more immortal, that is your success. All Nature is your congratulation, and you have cause momentarily to bless yourself.

Tao

The Tao Master Chaung-Tzu said it this way:

You never find happiness until you stop looking for it. If you ask "what ought to be done" and "what ought not to be done" in order to produce happiness, I answer that these questions do not have an answer. Yet at the same time, if I cease striving for happiness, the "right" and the "wrong" at once become apparent all by themselves. Contentment and well-being at once become possible the moment you cease to act with them in view, and if you practice non-doing, you will have both happiness and well-being.

The Sages say that this is becoming like Nature: it doesn't have anything to do, it just is. That is why it is a blessing to all. Just as we are part of the Tao, we are part of Nature. The more we are like it the more we are blessed.

Thoreau

After a still winter night I awoke with the impression that some question had been put to me: what – how – when – where?

But there was dawning Nature, in whom all creatures live, looking in at my broad windows with serene and satisfied face, and no question on *her* lips.

Nature puts no questions and answers none which we mortals ask. I awoke to an answered question, to Nature and daylight.

Tao

Nature asks no questions because it simply is what it is, and it does what it does. It is a great example of the idea of not-doing. Nature doesn't "do" rain; it rains when it rains. Nature is. To be like Nature, be.

Thoreau

The first sparrow of spring! The year beginning with younger hope than ever! I found myself suddenly neighbor to the birds; not by having imprisoned one, but having caged myself near them.

I once had a sparrow alight upon my shoulder for a moment while I was hoeing in a village garden, and I felt I was more distinguished by that circumstance than I should have been by any epaulet I could have worn.

The nighthawk circled overhead in the sunny afternoons, graceful and slender, like ripples caught up from the pond, as leaves are raised by the wind to float in the heavens; such kindredship is in Nature.

Tao

The elements of Nature reflect each other. A rock, a stone, a boulder and a mountain have the same patterns despite the difference in size. Veins look the same in arms and leaves, and both look like a river seen from space. This indicates what Chuang Tzu saw when he wrote: "He who regards all things as one is a companion of Nature." This is evidence of the truth of the Tao because the similarities of different forms reveal the deep, mysterious interconnectivity of the world.

Thoreau

The winds which passed over my dwelling were such as sweep over the ridges and mountains, bearing the broken strains, or celestial parts only, of terrestrial music.

The morning wind forever blows, the poem of creation is uninterrupted; but few are the ears that hear it.

Tao

Those that hear the poem of creation sense it everywhere.

Without going outside his door, you can be one with everything under the sky; without looking out from his window, one experiences the Tao.

The Seeker can see it inside of everything and everyone, to feel it as the energy of everything and everyone. To become a Sage is to merge into everything and everyone.

Thoreau

    It would be well perhaps if we were to spend more of our days and nights without any obstruction between us and the celestial bodies, if the poet did not speak so much from under a roof, or the saint dwell there so long.

    Birds do not sing in caves, nor do doves cherish their innocence in dovecots.

    Waiting at evening on the hill-tops for the sky to fall that I might catch something, though I never catch much, and that would dissolve again in the sun.

Tao

It is difficult to find natural rhythms without being out in Nature. Is there a more serene place than the woods? Learning to calm down clears the way for the inner voice. This work is the beginning of attuning the self to Nature and the Tao. Chuang Tzu said, "He who knows the activities of Nature lives according to Nature."

Being in Nature is being close to the Tao. As Thoreau understood, it can be felt but not captured: "Meet it, you cannot see its face. Follow it, you cannot see its back." Perhaps we cannot see its outside because we live inside Nature and the Tao.

Thoreau

No weather interfered with my walks. I frequently tramped eight or ten miles through the deepest snow to keep an appointment with a beech tree, or a yellow-birch, or an old acquaintance among the pines. Shall I not have intelligence with the earth? Am I not partly leaves and vegetable mold myself?

There is nothing inorganic. The earth is living poetry like the leaves of a tree, which precede flowers and fruit, a living earth.

Melt your metals and cast them in the most beautiful molds you can; they will never excite me like the forms which this molten earth flows out into.

Heaven is under our feet as well as over our heads.

Tao

Seeing the world this way is like seeing the Tao in all things, and beginning to understand the proper order:

Man follows the laws of earth; Earth follows the laws of heaven; Heaven follows the laws of Tao; Tao follows the laws of its intrinsic nature.

Thus, following the Tao means following the primal force. The Seeker becoming attuned to the Tao is attached to the greatest power there is.

Thoreau

 I love to see that Nature is so rife with life that myriads can be afforded to be sacrificed and suffered to prey on one another; that tender organizations can be so serenely squashed out of existence like pulp, tadpoles which herons gobble up, and tortoises and toads run over in the road. With the liability to accident, we must see how little account is to be made of it.

 The impression made on a wise man is that of universal innocence. Poison is not poisonous after all, nor are any wounds fatal.

Tao

An integral part of Taoism, though not unique to this philosophy, is that death is part of life, even though it can be personally painful. Thoreau saw that life and creation had such abundance that even multiple instances of death cannot blunt it. Lao-Tzu agrees, for "in harmony with the Tao all creatures flourish together, endlessly repeating themselves, endlessly renewed."

All creatures are part of the universal one, and Sages can "view the parts with compassion, because we understand the whole." This compassion is important, since even in the light of universal abundance, death is still tragic. It is a comfort to know that those who are no longer with us are still a part of the Tao, and thus immortal.

Thoreau

The wildest scenes had become unaccountably familiar. I found myself ranging the woods, like a half-starved hound, with a strange abandonment, seeking some venison that I might devour, and no morsel could have been too savage for me.

I caught a glimpse of a woodchuck stealing across my path, and I felt a strange thrill of savage delight, and was strongly tempted to seize and devour him raw; not that I was hungry then, except for the wildness that he represented.

I found in myself, and still find, an instinct toward a higher, spiritual life, and another toward a primitive and savage one, and I reverence them both.

Tao

The unity between the high and the low, the great and small, the savage and civilized reflects the great unity represented by Yin and Yang. It is sad that this symbol has become somewhat clichéd, since it is such a simple illustration of a great concept that reality is the merging of all into one, and one becoming all. Since all things are one, all things contain elements of each other.

Thoreau sees in man the melding of the animal and the divine, and it is wise to honor each one, and respect their balance.

If we are all part animal, then who should be looked down on? If we are all part divine, then who can say they are better?

Thoreau

    Of all the characters I have known, perhaps Walden Pond wears the best, and best preserves its purity.

    It is itself unchanged, the same waters my youthful eyes fell on; all the change is in me.

    The pure Walden water is mingled with the sacred water of the Ganges. Sympathy with the fluttering alder and poplar leaves almost takes away my breath; yet, like the lake, my serenity is rippled but not ruffled.

Tao

Walden Pond became a symbol to Thoreau of the divine purity at the source of all things. Water is a major symbol of the Tao:

> *The highest goodness is like water. Water is good to all things but does not contend. It stays in places which others despise. Therefore it is near Tao.*

Water reminds us to remain humble, to see obstacles as guides, to flow, and to nourish all things and help them grow.

Thoreau

This small lake was of most value as a neighbor in the intervals of a gentle rain storm in August, when, both air and water being perfectly still, but the sky overcast, mid-afternoon had all the serenity of evening.

A lake like this is never smoother than at such a time; and the clear portion of the air above it being shallow and darkened by clouds, the water, full of light and reflections, becomes a lower heaven itself so much the more important.

Once it chanced that I stood in the very abutment of a rainbow's arch, which filled the lower stratum of the atmosphere, tingeing the grass and leaves around, and dazzling me as if I looked through colored crystal. It was a lake of rainbow light, in which, for a short while, I lived like a dolphin.

These were the shrines I visited both summer and winter.

Tao

Thoreau saw Nature as the scripture of the Divine. This is because Nature is the perfect result of the great power in the universe.

It is no mistake that Thoreau found his serenity in Nature. It serves as the most direct guide to the rhythms of the universe. The patterns and cycles are laid bare for all to see; all Thoreau had to do was understand he was part of it to begin to grasp his own repeating ways. In this way, he began to gain control of himself, to understand his world, and to tap into his power.

Thoreau

I was suddenly sensible of such sweet and beneficent society in Nature, in the very pattering of the drops, and in every sound and sight around my house, an infinite and unaccountable friendliness all at once like an atmosphere sustaining me, as made the fancied advantages of human neighborhood insignificant.

Every little pine needle expanded and swelled with sympathy and befriended me. I was aware of the presence of something kindred to me, even in scenes which we are accustomed to call wild and dreary, and also that the nearest of blood to me and humanest was not a person nor a villager, that I thought no place could ever be strange to me again.

Tao

This is the climax of Thoreau's life in the woods. He has finally found his home, and it is Nature. Not simply in the woods, by a pond, but in the great Nature that all are part of. This oneness is what anyone looking for peace, or searching for the Tao longs to feel. How to find such companionship without building a cabin in the woods? Here:

> *Therefore Tao gives Life to all beings,*
> *It nourishes and makes them grow,*
> *It rears them and perfects them,*
> *It sustains, feeds, and protects them.*
> *It gives them Life, but does not possess them.*
> *It gives them activity, but does not depend on them.*
> *It urges them to grow, but does not rule them.*

Thoreau

Not until we are completely lost, or turned round, for a man needs only to be turned round once with his eyes shut in this world to be lost, do we appreciate the vastness and strangeness of Nature.

Not until we are lost, not till we have lost the world, do we begin to find ourselves, and realize where we are and the infinite extent of our relations.

Tao

As the Tao tells us:

Therefore he who regards the world as he does his own body can govern the world. He who loves the world as he does his own body can be entrusted with the world.

If all is one, then all can be beloved. Feeling this way, imagine how much each moment is transformed, and we can truly love all things and accept the genuine love from all things.

Thoreau

Sometimes, after staying in a village parlor till the family had retired, I returned to the woods, and, partly with a view to the next day's dinner, spent the hours of midnight fishing from a boat by moonlight, serenaded by owls and foxes, and hearing, from time to time, the creaking note of some unknown bird close at hand.

These experiences were very memorable and valuable to me, surrounded sometimes by thousands of small perch and shiners, dimpling the surface with their tails in the moonlight, and communicating by a long flaxen line with mysterious nocturnal fishes, now and then feeling a slight vibration along it, indicative of some life prowling about its extremity.

It was very queer, especially in dark nights, when your thoughts had wandered to vast and cosmological themes in other spheres, to feel this faint jerk, which came to interrupt your dreams and link you to Nature again. It seemed as if I might next cast my line upward into the air, as well as downward into this element which was scarcely more dense. Thus I caught two fishes with one hook.

Tao

As Thoreau fishes and ponders the mysteries of the universe, a tug on his line brings him back to the world and its countless objects. It is in all the individual forms, the foxes, the birds, the fish and the trees, which Thoreau gained his understanding of the universe. The great oneness is made up of infinite individual versions. The fish on the end of his hook reminds Thoreau that this miracle is not just to be pondered; it is to be lived.

Thoreau

As I was bending my steps again to the pond, my haste to catch pickerel appeared for an instant trivial to me who had been sent to school and college.

But as I ran down the hill toward the reddening west, with the rainbow over my shoulder, and some faint tinkling sounds borne to my ear through the cleansed air, my Good Genius seemed to say "Go fish and hunt far and wide day by day – farther and wider – and rest by many brooks and hearth-sides without misgiving."

Remember thy creator in the days of thy youth. Rise free from care before the dawn and seek adventures. Let the noon find thee by other lakes, and the night overtake thee everywhere at home.

Tao

In chapter 26 of the *Tao Te Ching,* Lao-tzu tells us that "The Master travels all day without leaving home." Clearly, both understood that a person open to the world, and thus open to the Tao, can never be anywhere but where they belong.

Thoreau

    The light which puts out our eyes is darkness to us. Only that day dawns to which we are awake. There is more day to dawn. The sun is but a morning star.
    If we feel the influence of the spring of springs arousing us, we will rise to a higher and more ethereal life.

Tao

The awakening to oneness, the embracing of cyclical Nature opens up the path to the divine. Living in the Tao means being inside the source of power, and it means to be ever refreshed and renewed. To become a Sage, Chuang Tzu tells us, means having:

> *The sun and moon by his side and the universe under his arm. He blends everything into a harmonious whole. He blends the disparities of ten thousand years into one complete purity. All things are blended like this and mutually involve each other.*

If the power of all is also the power of one, then action that is in harmony with this power is supported by the universe.

Thoreau

I know of no more encouraging fact than the unquestionable ability of man to elevate his life by conscious endeavor.

It is something to be able to paint a particular picture, or to carve a statue, and so to make a few objects beautiful; but it is far more glorious to carve and paint the very atmosphere and medium through which we look, which morally we can do.

Every man is tasked to make his life, even in its details, worthy of the contemplation of his most elevated and critical hour. To affect the quality of the day, that is the highest of arts.

Tao

Thoreau makes right action and right living part of his daily practice. Each day, each moment can be refined to such an extent that the Sage can look back without needing to judge or criticize. The *Tao Te Ching* lays down the path to such action:

> *To act without acting; to conduct affairs without being troubled. Regard the small as great; regard the few as many. Manage the difficult while it is easy. Manage the great while it is small.*

To become such a Sage takes practice. This doesn't contradict the spirit of the above passage, because effortless work comes only after refining action. Embodying these ideas, even in a limited way, moves the Seeker further within enlightenment.

Thoreau

Ice begins with delicate crystal leaves. The feathers and wings of birds are still drier and thinner leaves. The whole tree itself is but one leaf, and rivers are still vaster leaves whose pulp is intervening earth, and town and cities are the ova of insects in their axils.

The very globe continually transcends and translates itself, and becomes winged in its orbit. *Next* to us the grandest laws are continually being executed. *Next* to us is not the workman we have hired, with whom we love so well to talk, but the workman whose work we are.

God himself culminates in the present moment, and will never by more divine in the lapse of all the ages. Nearest to all things is that power which fashions their being.

Tao

This mysterious, miraculous harmony is a source of insight into the Great Tao, which "flows through all things, inside and outside, and returns to the origin of all things." In his own way, Thoreau saw that each small thing, each piece of the Tao, is simultaneously a form of the Tao, an example of the Tao, and the Tao itself. Remembering this assures those on the path that they are already all they need to be, and have access to all the power they will ever need. The secret is becoming open to what is already in and around us.

Thoreau

I desire to speak somewhere *without* bounds; like a man in a waking moment, to men in their waking moments; for I am convinced that I could not exaggerate enough even to lay the foundation of a true expression. Who that has heard a strain of music feared then he should speak extravagantly any more forever?

In view of the future or possible, we should live quite laxly and undefined in front, our outlines dim and misty on that side.

We need to witness our own limits transgressed, and some life pasturing freely where we never wander. The universe is wider than our views of it.

Tao

The ancient Master said:

Other people have a purpose; I alone don't know. I drift like a wave on the ocean, I blow as aimless as the wind. Ordinary men look bright and intelligent, while I alone am dull and confused. I seem to be carried about as on the sea, drifting as if I had nowhere to rest.

Having goals and purpose is wise, but as these philosophers say, it is unwise to set ideas in stone. Let the moment be the guide. Be unafraid to wander off the planned path if another, better path opens up. It may meander its way to the original objective, but the wanderer may find something unexpected and divine along the way.

Thoreau

I have been anxious to improve the nick of time, and notch it on my stick too; to stand on the meeting of two eternities, the past and the future, which is precisely the present moment; to toe that line.

I would fish in the sky, whose bottom is pebbly with stars. I cannot count one. I know not the first letter of the alphabet. I have always been regretting that I was not as wise as the day I was born.

Time is but the stream I go fishing in. I see the sandy bottom and detect how shallow it is. Its thin current slides away, but eternity remains.

Tao

Thoreau gets as close as a thinker can to expressing the nature of eternity and the everlasting moment. Time, like all aspects of the Tao, contains both the oneness of the infinite as well as the myriad individual moments that make up the eternal.

These kinds of thoughts help remind the Sage to be present. A Sage, experiencing oneness with the Tao:

> *May be compared to an infant. His bones are*
> *frail, his sinews tender, but his grasp is strong.*
> *He may cry all day without growing hoarse;*
> *it means that he is in perfect harmony.*

The wisdom of a baby is an automatic oneness. A baby's hunger is not selfish, its smiles are not generous; both are genuine, which is why we feed it freely and take so much joy from its happiness. The baby lives in the moment, without preconceived notions, because it cannot be any other way.

Thoreau

The man who does not believe that each day contains an earlier, more sacred and auroral hour, has despaired of life, and is pursuing a descending and darkening way.

Little is to be expected of that day, if it can be called a day, to which we are not awakened by our Genius, are not awakened by our own newly-acquired force and aspirations from within, accompanied by the undulations of celestial music, and a fragrance filling the air – to a higher life than we fell asleep from; and thus the darkness bears its fruit, and proves itself to be good, no less than the light.

Tao

Days and nights lived in the Tao gives access to more of its power.

Tao is infinite.
If we use It, we find It inexhaustible,
Deep!
It rounds our angles. It unravels our difficulties. It harmonizes our Light. It brings our atoms into Unity.

Each fully lived moment is also practice for greater days, because it was spent living in the Tao. Thus, each one of these moments makes a greater day, and brings the Seeker another step closer to becoming a Sage.

Thoreau

We must learn to reawaken and keep ourselves awake, by an infinite expectation of the dawn.

Morning is when I am awake and there is dawn in me. To be awake is to be alive. To him whose elastic and vigorous thought keeps pace with the sun, the day is a perpetual morning.

I have never yet met a man who was quite awake. How could I have looked him in the face?

Tao

The ever-present morning is a symbol of the constant, inexhaustible nature of the Tao. To be like Thoreau is to have this morning inside, to be fresh and awake no matter the time of day.

Tapped into the power of reality, living in the first light, a Sage is ever awakened to this power. It is always there, and always more than enough. Who could look at a face that shines with the light of the sun? Others will have to turn their faces from the radiance, though the glow warms them and lights their way.

Thoreau

This is the only way, we say; but there are as many ways as there can be drawn radii from one center. All change is a miracle to contemplate; but it is a miracle which is taking place every instant.

I love to weigh, to settle, to gravitate toward that which most strongly and rightfully attracts me; not hang by the beam of the scale and try to weigh less, not suppose a case, but take the case that is; to travel the only path I can, and that on which no power can resist me.

If I seem to boast more than is becoming, my excuse is that I brag for humanity rather than for myself.

Tao

Lao-tzu asked:

Who can make muddy water clear? Let it settle, and it will gradually become clear. Who can remain unmoving until the right action arises by itself?

With the strength of patience and the force of clarity, we settle to where the action comes to us fluidly, becoming an irresistible power. It is hard to stop someone marching to the orders of the universe.

Thoreau

With thinking we may be beside ourselves in a sane sense. By a conscious effort of the mind we can stand aloof from actions and their consequences; and all things, good and bad, go by us like a torrent. We are not wholly involved in Nature. I may be either the driftwood in the stream, or Indra in the sky looking down on it.

I know myself as a human entity; the scene of thoughts and affections; and am sensible of a certain doubleness by which I can stand as remote from myself as from another. However intense my experience, I am conscious of the presence and criticism of a part of me, which is not a part of me, but spectator, sharing no experience, but taking note of it; and that is no more I than it is you.

Tao

Just as "we are not wholly involved in Nature," we also have a certain separateness from the Tao. Perhaps Thoreau is experiencing the perspective of the Great Tao, observing and guiding the little piece of Tao that he is as a man. "The Tao is like uncarved block of wood, which can be made into many utensils."

Thoreau is experiencing being the utensils and the block simultaneously. He is the man that came from something: call it Nature, God, the Tao. The created comes from it, is connected to it, is apart from it, and is a part of it. Calming the spirit and the mind opens the connection wider. Understanding the self as a utensil, attuned to Nature and the Tao, you can use yourself to accomplish what is right and good. Understanding where you came from reminds you to access its power, as it is also your own.

Thoreau

If you stand right fronting and face to face to a fact, you will see the sun glimmer on both its surfaces as if it were a scimitar, and feel its sweet edge dividing you through the heart and marrow, and so you will happily conclude your mortal career.

Tao

The term "fact" is interchangeable with "Truth" or "Tao." This does not need to be some vast cosmic fact; it can be a simple realization about an important truth of life. Such realizations change a person's world, metaphorically ending one existence by giving birth to a new life.

Thoreau

    It is remarkable how easily and insensibly we fall into a particular route, and make a beaten track for ourselves. The surface of the earth is soft and impressible by the feet of men; and so with the paths which the mind travels. How worn and dusty, then, must be the highways of the world, how deep the ruts of tradition and conformity!

    I left the woods for as good a reason as I went there. Perhaps it seemed to me that I had several more lives to live, and could not spare any more time for that one.

Tao

It's amazing to contemplate that Thoreau would walk away from an experience that had taught him so much. But if he hadn't, it would prove he didn't learn the lessons it taught him. For:

> *The Master allows things to happen.*
> *She shapes events as they come.*
> *She steps out of the way*
> *and lets the Tao speak for itself.*

Know when something is done. Clinging to things robs them of whatever wonder and beauty they once had. True things will not wear away. What Thoreau has learned is not contingent on where he lives. It is in him now, with him always, and can never be taken. Ideas so profound, so ever present, that all can learn from them. These ideas won't create more ruts because they are ideas of flexibility, suppleness, and adaptability, which give access to the power of change.

Thoreau

These may be but the spring months in the life of the race. We are acquainted with the mere pellicle of a globe on which we live. Most have not delved six feet beneath the surface, nor leaped as many above it. We know not where we are. Besides, we are sound asleep nearly half our time.

Who knows what beautiful and winged life, whose egg has been buried for ages under many concentric layers of woodenness in the dead dry life of society, may unexpectedly come forth to enjoy its perfect summer at last!

Tao

Despite all the power and knowledge he has gained, Thoreau understands there is so much more. Each step on the Sage's path tends to open up realizations that there is still a higher, greater life than the one so far achieved. Chuang-tzu said:

The mind remains undetermined in the great Void. Here the highest knowledge is unbounded. So when we speak of 'limits', we remain confined to limited things. The limit of the unlimited is called 'fullness.' The limitlessness of the limited is called 'emptiness.' Tao is the source of both. But it is itself neither fullness nor emptiness.

Awareness of limits gives insight into how they can be crossed. Belief in the limitless gives access to its power. The unlimited greatness of the Tao holds us inside it and grants us access to its bottomless well.

Thoreau

I learned this, at least, from my experiment: that if one advances confidently in the direction of his dreams, and endeavors to live the life which he has imagined, he will meet with success unexpected in common hours. He will put some things behind, will pass an invisible boundary; new, universal, and more liberal laws will begin to establish themselves around and within him; or the old laws be expanded, and interpreted in his favor in a more liberal sense, and he will live with the license of a higher order of beings.

In proportion as he simplifies his life, the laws of the universe will appear less complex, and solitude will not be solitude, nor weakness weakness.

If you have built castles in the air, your work need not be lost; that is where they should be. Now put the foundations under them.

Tao

The greatest power, the one that lasts, is harmony. Struggle isn't struggle because it is necessary; problems are not problems but training for success. The Seeker can eliminate worry and doubt by beginning to realize:

Because he beleives in himself, he doesn't try to convince others. Because he is content with himself, he doesn't need others' approval. Because he accepts himself, the whole world accepts him.

This is the simplicity that Thoreau sought. Following the Tao means living the freedom of its laws: creativity, conservation, recharging, endless strength and durability. Thus, the Seeker becomes the Sage by sinking into the power that has always been there, by becoming the Tao and acting as one with the laws of the universe.

Printed in Great Britain
by Amazon